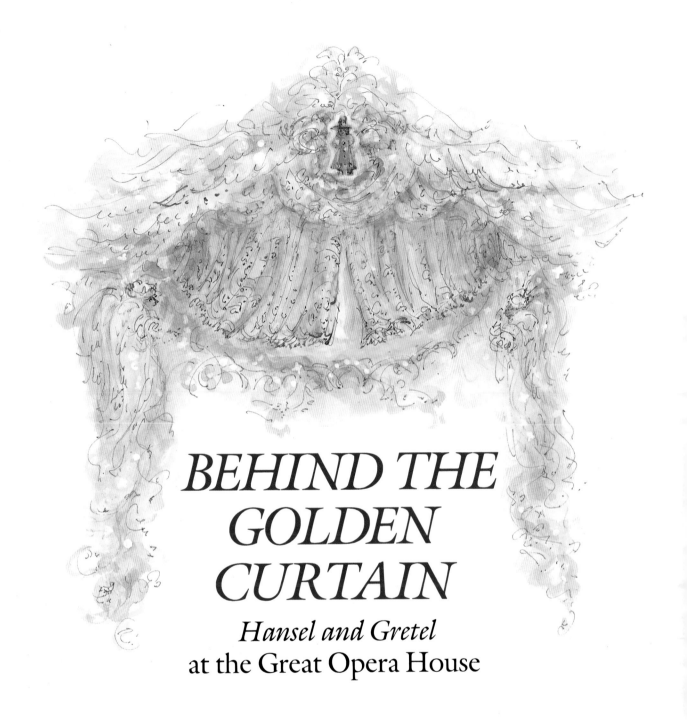

BEHIND THE GOLDEN CURTAIN

Hansel and Gretel
at the Great Opera House

E. Lee Spruyt

FOUR WINDS PRESS

NEW YORK

Dedicated to
the many magical yet hidden people
at the Great Opera House
and the Metropolitan Opera Guild.

Special thanks to Robert O'Hearn, Fay, Harry, and Meredith.

Copyright © 1986 by E. Lee Spruyt
All rights reserved. No part of this book may be reproduced
or transmitted in any form or by any means, electronic or
mechanical, including photocopying, recording or by any
information storage and retrieval system, without
permission in writing from the Publisher.
Four Winds Press
Macmillan Publishing Company
866 Third Avenue, New York, NY 10022
Collier Macmillan Canada, Inc.
Printed and bound in Japan
First American Edition
10 9 8 7 6 5 4 3 2 1
The text of this book is set in 14 pt. Galliard.
The illustrations are rendered in pen-and-ink and watercolor.
Library of Congress Cataloging-in-Publication Data
Spruyt, E. Lee.
Behind the golden curtain.
Summary: Describes both onstage and backstage
preparations for the opening night of an opera
production.
1. Opera – Production and direction – Juvenile literature.
2. Humperdinck, Engelbert, 1854-1921. Hänsel
und Gretel – Juvenile literature. [1. Opera – Production
and direction] I. Title.
MT955.S687 1986   782.1'07'3   85-15869
ISBN 0-02-786400-6

It is five-thirty on a cold, rainy morning. Already people are traveling to the great opera house. Some come by subway or bus. Others ride bicycles or drive their cars. A few even come by ferry. All these people will enter through the warmly lit stage door and work long hours before returning home. For tonight is the opening production of the opera *Hansel and Gretel*.

An opera is a story told through music. Many years ago the German composer Engelbert Humperdinck thought that a fairy tale might make a good opera. He chose *Hansel and Gretel* by the Brothers Grimm.

Nearly everyone knows the story: One day, looking for wild strawberries, Hansel and Gretel lose their way in the forest. Hungry and afraid, they come upon the most wonderful cottage they have ever seen. It is made entirely of gingerbread, bright juicy candies, and colored frosting, and it is surrounded by a fence of Gingerbread Children.

The cottage looks delicious, but woe to anyone who takes a bite! Hansel cannot resist, and he and Gretel are captured by the witch who lives within. She means to eat Hansel for dinner, but Gretel out-smarts her and pops the witch into her own oven. Hansel and Gretel free the Gingerbread Children from the witch's spell, and they all live happily ever after.

Engelbert Humperdinck asked a writer, Adelheid Wette, to create the *libretto,* or words, for his opera. Then he set the libretto to music. And he was right: The story of Hansel and Gretel does make a good opera. It is fun to listen to, and fun to watch, for it is filled with magical effects.

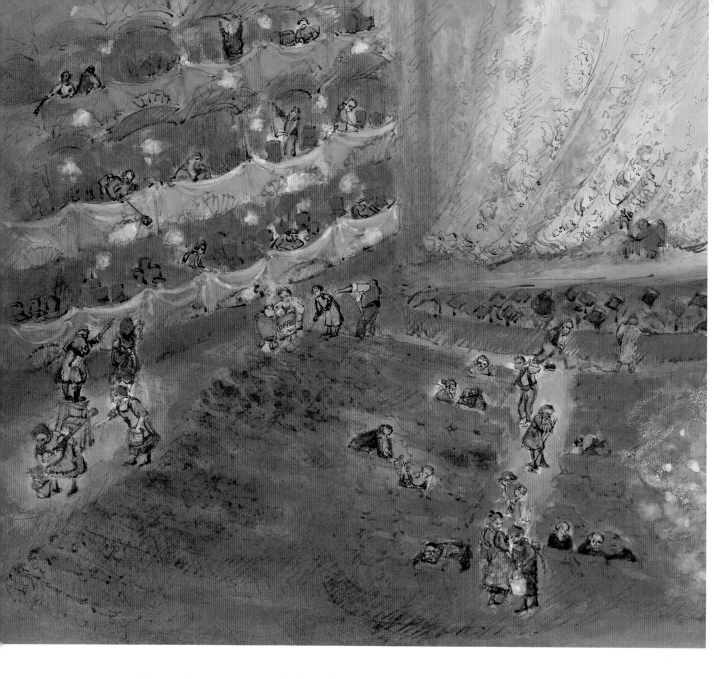

Hansel and Gretel has been performed many times. Tonight, on the stage of the great opera house, it will be performed again. The curtain will rise at eight o'clock, and musicians, singers, dancers, actors, and even a cat will dazzle and delight the audience. But now, very early in the morning, vacuum cleaners are whining and hammers are banging. Everyone is talking in morning whispers and there's the smell of fresh coffee.

The crystal chandeliers are lowered to be carefully cleaned. Their glass prisms sparkle, making rainbows in the dimness of the theater. Slowly the chandeliers are drawn back up to the ceiling. The "bulbman" hikes from the Orchestra to the Family Circle, reaching up with his long basket stick to unscrew and replace all burned-out light bulbs.

Outside the opera house, a man stretches against gusts of wind to paste a sign on the poster for tonight's production. It reads SOLD OUT. There are no tickets left.

By late morning the director, who is in charge of everything that happens onstage, has arrived. Then come the musicians of the orchestra, a group of dancers, and the "principals," or lead singers. They will perform the star roles of Hansel, Gretel, their parents, and Rosina Dainty Mouth, the wicked witch.

The Children of the Chorus, who play Gingerbread Children, and the "supers," actors who have small, non-singing roles, all arrive.

Then, watched carefully by the General Manager of the opera house, the director, and his stage director, the musicians, singers, dancers, and supers begin their final rehearsals of *Hansel and Gretel*.

Meanwhile, backstage people are carrying on with their special jobs.

In the lighting switchboard, or master control room, behind the audience at the very back of the theater, electricians are studying the lighting design for tonight's performance. From behind their soundproof window, using computers and other devices that are connected to lights around the theater and stage, they can create the illusion of day or nighttime. As they run through the light changes for *Hansel and Gretel,* all sorts of switches and colored lights flash on and off.

In the electric shop, illusions and special effects are created. In *Hansel and Gretel,* there will be blinking stars, a cuckoo calling, even silver angel dust. The electric shop's finest creation is the witch's magic oven that will explode in billows of smoke.

The scenic artists of the scenic shop carry out the stage designer's plans. If those plans call for a deep forest, the scenic designers will create one. They paint all scenery and backdrops, as well as some costumes.

Amid the smell of paint and glue, some scenic artists use brushes attached to long bamboo sticks so they can paint freely while walking over yards of canvas stretched and stapled to the floor. Or they stand on the paint bridge high over the stage, painting on huge canvases that can be moved up and down the height of two or three floors. For *Hansel and Gretel,* all sorts of materials and methods have been used to get many effects.

The stage designer has also worked with the prop department. The prop department has a full collection of handy things like jeweled goblets, eyeglasses, brightly colored umbrellas, dishes, swords, and shields. What they don't have, they make. For *Hansel and Gretel,* they have provided rocks, a cuckoo, Rosina Dainty Mouth's magic wand and broomstick, and even a baked wicked witch. Some props are real, some are fake, but all are needed to create illusions on the stage.

The carpentry shop builds things that people can get on top of, into, and over. Everywhere are the sounds of hammers and saws and the smell of sawdust. For the scenery they build, the carpenters always try to use lightweight materials such as plastic foam and fiber glass. Less weight helps the stagehands take scenery on- and offstage quickly. It also helps when the opera company goes "on the road" all over the world, and scenery has to be packed up and transported.

In one corner of the carpentry shop, last-minute repairs are being made to the Gingerbread House. In another, large frames, called *flats,* are being constructed for a different production. Fireproof canvas will be stretched over the frames to be painted later by the scenic department.

Sewing machines are humming and purring in the costume shop. Here, a large staff of expert seamstresses and tailors construct costumes from sketches made by the costume designer. The costumes must be lightweight so the performers can move easily and stay cool under the hot stage lights. Costumes must last from ten to fifteen years.

The storerooms of the costume shop are full of fabrics, trimmings, bright fake jewels, boots, shoes, hats, and even padded shapes to make fat bellies. The costume designer also works with the wig and makeup staff to get the effects she wants to go with her costumes. In *Hansel and Gretel* the wicked witch presents a special problem for the make-up artists: She must be able to sing with a fake chin and a fake long nose with a wart.

At three o'clock in the afternoon, rehearsals are over. The performers go home to rest and have dinner. Backstage, the activity quickens. Costumes are ironed, mended, labeled with each performer's name, and laid out, ready to be put on, with the help of the wardrobe dressers. The head-dresses for the Creatures of the Forest are placed in the dressing rooms, and fourteen angel costumes are carefully hung and checked.

Ezekiel, a tiger cat, is brought backstage in his box. Like other professional animals, he will be paid for his performance. Tonight, he'll appear onstage in Act I, as Hansel and Gretel's beloved pet.

It is six o'clock, two hours before curtain time. The musicians and the cast of singers, dancers, and supers return through the stage door to get into their costumes and makeup.

Last-minute repairs are made; wigs are carefully fitted. The stage crews push the scenery into place.

Through the bustle, the singers' strong, rich voices can be heard. They are "warming up" before the performance.

At seven o'clock, the great opera house lights up, glowing in the winter night. Snow is whirling in the wind. From every part of the city, people are coming by bus, subway, car, taxi, and limousine. They are members of the audience, hurrying to the opening-night production of *Hansel and Gretel*.

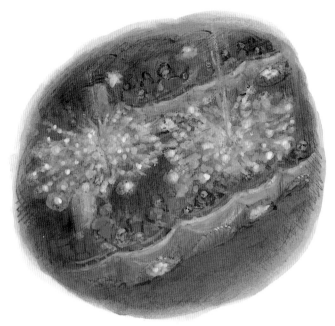

Inside, the chandeliers have been lowered to give the audience more light as they find their seats with the help of ushers.

Some do not have seats at all; they are called *standees*. Many are students. For very little money, they will watch the performance standing, either in the back of the opera house or in the "peanut gallery," located behind the top seats of the house.

Electricians are climbing into the light boxes near the top of the ceiling. They are like small islands glowing in the clouds. This is where many spotlights and slide projections come from.

The prompter, whose job is to guide and direct nervous singers if they forget their cues, climbs into his hooded box, center stage behind the footlights. Inside is a phone to call the stage manager and a television screen.

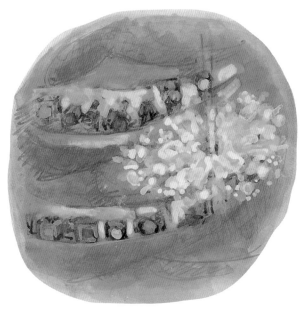

The General Manager of the opera house rushes through a secret passage from his office to his special box. He waits anxiously for the orchestra to begin playing.

The musicians hurry to their seats in the orchestra pit. They begin to tune up their instruments. The sparkling chandeliers, glittering like stars, slowly dim and move up to the ceiling. From the audience there are *ooh*'s and *aah*'s. The concertmaster steps up to the podium and asks for an "A" using his violin. Other instruments join in.

Behind the golden curtain there is complete silence. The stage has just been sprayed with water to settle dust, which is bad for the singers' voices. The cast have taken their places. The angels, who are really dancers, are ready to fly. The Dew Fairy waits quietly along with the Sandman, Creatures of the Forest, the Gingerbread Children, and a huge Spider with wiggling legs. Stagehands standing in the shadows are ready to push trees onto the darkened

stage for the forest scene. Everyone—cast and crew—is watching for *cues,* or directions, from the stage manager.

Offstage, the stage director is sitting in front of his console. He watches the clock and checks his prompt book, which has all the cues for this production. He also checks two television screens, one that watches the stage and one that watches the podium, where the conductor of the orchestra stands.

At eight o'clock, the conductor climbs onto the podium. The stage manager gives the signal that means "curtain." The house darkens. The audience is still. The conductor raises his baton and the orchestra begins to play.

Slowly, the golden curtains part.

Framed by the golden curtains, the story of Hansel and Gretel is magically enacted through music, dance, and wonderful special effects. In the beginning of Act II, the audience gasps in wonder as the glowing Gingerbread House, on a huge elevator below stage, moves slowly into view through the mist.

Although the opera has lasted over two hours, it seems to end too soon. The witch has been outsmarted, the Gingerbread Children freed. The entire company—the conductor, performers, the director, the stage director, members of the orchestra, and stagehands—take bows together. As the audience cheers and claps, flowers are given to Hansel and Gretel, or thrown on the stage. The singer playing Rosina Dainty Mouth is booed and hissed, but it is all in fun.

The golden curtain closes. People begin to leave the opera house, happily humming the music and talking excitedly about the performance. The houselights come up and slowly the asbestos fire curtain creeps down. Calling goodnight to one another, happy with the success of the opening, the cast and crew of *Hansel and Gretel* leave by the stage door to go home.

But the great opera house never sleeps. The night crew is already hard at work, getting the stage ready for tomorrow's rehearsal and tomorrow night's performance.